EASY DAY HIKES IN YOSEMITE

Twenty Enjoyable Trails

by Deborah J. Durkee
Illustrations by Fiona King

YOSEMITE ASSOCIATION
YOSEMITE NATIONAL PARK, CALIFORNIA

To Jonathan, Melissa, Julia, Andrew and Olivia who discovered these trails with me.

Yosemite Association
P.O. Box 230
El Portal, CA 95318

The Yosemite Association initiates and supports interpretive, educational, research, scientific, and environmental programs in Yosemite National Park, in cooperation with the National Park Service. Authorized by Congress, the Association provides services and direct financial support in order to promote park stewardship and enrich the visitor experience.

To learn more about our activities or for information about membership, please write to the address above, call (209) 379-2646 or visit our web site at http://yosemite.org

To purchase additional copies of this book or any other Yosemite-related publications, visit the Yosemite Association's Internet store at http://www.yosemitestore.com

Design by Robin Weiss Graphic Design, San Carlos, CA.

TABLE OF CONTENTS

ABOUT THIS BOOK

A visit to Yosemite is really not complete until you have wandered into its quiet wilderness and experienced nature undisturbed. You don't have to go on a lengthy backpack trip to do this, however. Many trails begin at a road and lead you to especially scenic spots only a mile or two along. This guide is designed to help you find those trails. The hikes are short enough to be done in a day (including a drive to the trailhead from other parts of the park). The trails are also either to or through significantly picturesque areas of the park.

Each hike is described in detail to give a clear idea of what kind of terrain you will cover and what interesting things you can expect to see. At the beginning of each description the round trip hiking distance is stated as well as a suggestion for how much time you should allow for the hike. The suggestion does not include the time you choose to stay at your destination but does include brief stops along the way for those who like to investigate things more closely. Each hike is categorized according to its level of difficulty. This categorization is based on the length and incline of the trail. However, the hikes included are all within the physical capabilities of families with young children.

Before You Go

If hiking is new to you, take time to read the following suggestions to help you plan your trip.

Visitor Center

A stop at a visitor center or ranger station before you hike will be helpful if you have any questions about the condition of the trail. In early summer some trails are still covered with snow or are very muddy. Also you can get extensive information from the rangers on how to prepare backcountry water for drinking, how to handle sanitation needs, and even what to do if you meet a bear along the way!

Shoes and Clothes

Wear the sturdiest shoes you have. Walking in sandals will make the trip uncomfortable. Keep in mind while you dress that weather can change quickly in the mountains. Typically Yosemite's summer mornings and evenings are cool and afternoons are hot. However,

hikes to higher elevations or to vista points can be breezy any time of day. You may wish to bring an extra wrap.

Water and Food

In hot weather you will need to carry water and, depending on the length of the hike, you may want to bring lunch or snacks. If you are taking children with you on the hike, remember that their enthusiasm for wilderness travel will diminish quickly once they become hungry or thirsty. Some snacks children enjoy while hiking are GORP (Good Old Raisins and Peanuts—to which we add sunflower seeds and M&Ms), popped corn, granola bars, and dried or fresh fruit. (Remember to pack out your trash.)

Backcountry Sanitation

Few trails have bathrooms or pit toilets available. Be prepared with toilet paper and a small trowel. Observe park regulations which specify that human waste be buried at least one hundred feet from any water or trail, and six inches deep. It is important to safeguard the purity of the water supply.

First Aid

If you think to tuck a few bandages or bandaging supplies in your pocket you will be prepared to handle any occasional cuts and scrapes. A small container of insect repellent and of sun screen may also be worth carrying.

Extra Baggage

Depending on how much room you have in your pockets or day pack, any of the following will add to the enjoyment of your hike: identification books on plants, trees, rocks, butterflies, mammals, reptiles, etc., a hand lens for looking closely at tiny objects, binoculars, a camera, drawing supplies, fishing gear, and swimming suits.

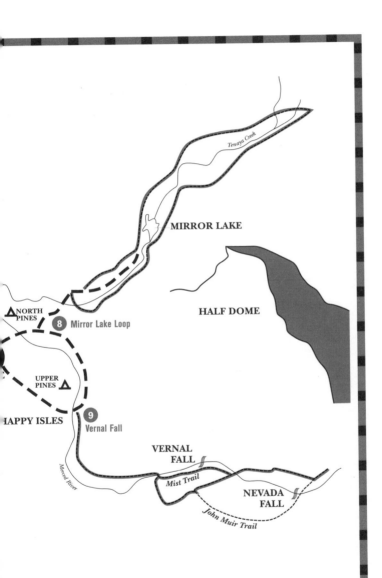

MIRROR LAKE

HALF DOME

NORTH
PINES

8 Mirror Lake Loop

UPPER
PINES

HAPPY ISLES

9 Vernal Fall

VERNAL
FALL

Mist Trail

NEVADA
FALL

John Muir Trail

Tenaya Creek

Merced River

> **YOSEMITE VALLEY**
> 2.8 miles | Easy | 2 hours

This trail connects several popular areas in the valley by way of a pleasant loop through Leidig Meadow. Included are a walk to the base of Yosemite Falls and stops at bridges over the Merced River, offering some exceptional views of Yosemite Valley's features.

Ride the shuttlebus to the Sentinel Bridge parking area (stop #11). As you walk across this bridge, stop to enjoy the famous view of Half Dome with the Merced River below. This is a popular place from which to photograph the famous landmark, especially when the river is at a low level in late summer and through winter. The view of Half Dome reflected in the quiet river is a memorable one.

Just over the bridge turn right on the paved walk towards the Yosemite Chapel. See if you can identify the four young sequoias on the opposite side of the road. Cross Southside Drive to the chapel, making a stop at this historic structure. It is the oldest building in the park still in use. It was built in 1879 at the southwest end of Leidig Meadow. Other structures erected in that area have since been moved or razed. In its present location, the chapel is used as an interdenominational place of worship.

Walk through the chapel parking area and continue along the trail leading away from the building. Follow along the edge of a large meadow and meet the trail running along the base of the south valley wall. Take the trail west (to the right) through a shady forest of cedar, maple, fir, and oak. The view of the meadow becomes obstructed by trees, while the sheer rock wall becomes visible to the left. Farther along, rugged Sentinel Rock towers above you. As the forest cover becomes less dense and the trail begins to parallel the road, watch for a parking area and picnic spot on the other side of Southside Drive. Cross the road at the crosswalk on the east end of this parking area. A paved path leads you through the picnic area and on to a wooden bridge across the Merced River.

An excellent view of Yosemite Falls awaits you at the bridge. Looking west from the bridge you see the Cathedral Rocks. To the south Sentinel Rock juts out from the ridge above, and to the east is the rounded top of North Dome.

Beyond the bridge, follow the path through Leidig Meadow toward Yosemite Lodge. Looking toward the eastern end of the valley, Half Dome, Clouds Rest, and the Royal Arches become visible.

A sandy beach along the Merced River is accessible from this trail.

The paved walk brings you to a road running through a developed housing area. Go right and at the first opportunity head straight to Northside Drive, where you should cross over to Sunnyside campground. Just beyond the information booth for the campground, catch the trail that heads up the hill. In about 100 yards you will come to the junction of the north valley trail with the Yosemite Falls trail. Follow the path to the east (to the right) where the sign reads ".6 mi to Lower Yosemite Fall."

This sandy trail is open and sunny. It winds along the base of the canyon wall where rock climbers often practice their skills. The route continues to the parking area below Yosemite Falls. A walk up the paved path to the base of the falls rewards you with a close-up view of Lower Yosemite Fall and, in the spring and early summer, a shower of mist.

At the east end of the parking area the trail continues over a footbridge parallel to the road. Keep to the right where the sign indicates "Stables 2.8," then cross another footbridge and follow the path back to Northside Drive. Cross the road and take the paved walk that heads south through the meadow.

The large building ahead was the home of Yosemite National Park superintendents until the 1980s. It was damaged in the flood of 1997, and probably will be torn down.

The trail through the meadow is lined with grass and bracken ferns that are mingled with flowers in the late spring. At the next trail junction you are presented with a choice of routes back to Sentinel Bridge. The path to the left leads directly to the parking area. The path to the right leads to a bridge that takes you back over the Merced River. Across this bridge, the trail leads you to Southside Drive near the chapel. Follow the paved walk to the left to re-cross Sentinel Bridge to your starting point.

MIRROR LAKE LOOP

| 4.8 miles | Moderate | 3½ hours |

Many people take the easy walk to Mirror Lake while in Yosemite Valley. Few, however, are aware that the trail beyond the lake offers a pleasant walk along Tenaya Creek as it runs down the narrow canyon and flows into Mirror Lake. Shuttle busses stop at the road to Mirror Lake during the summer; in winter you can begin your hike from the stables, walking east to the intersecting road to Mirror Lake.

Park visitors were once allowed to drive over this paved road all the way to the lake. Now it is off limits to vehicles—with the exception of park service trucks, cars with special permits for the handicapped, and bicyclists. Pit toilets near the parking area at the lake are still maintained for the use of visitors. The road takes you through a wooded area with a mixture of deciduous and evergreen trees. After crossing over Tenaya Creek on a stone bridge, the road follows the creek up an easy incline to Mirror Lake.

About .3 mile past the bridge you have the option of taking the footpath which branches off the road to the left. This parallels the main route and then rejoins it before the lake. You lose your view of the creek if you take the footpath, but gain greater solitude.

The appearance of Mirror Lake varies widely from season to season. In the spring it is at its most lake-like, then turns to a quiet, shallow pond in late summer and fall, and freezes in the deep of winter. Mirror Lake is in a state of transition as are other mountain lakes. Sand and debris are carried down the mountain ravines by streams running into Tenaya Creek. As the creek slows its pace on its course through the lake, the sediments are deposited. These deposits slowly are accumulating in the lake. Some day, instead of a lake, there will be a meadow here with a stream passing through it.

At any season of the year, the view of the massive granite formations reflected in the water is impressive. The most well-known of these is Half Dome, which seems to rise right out of the lake. At the east end of the lake, the cliff-like feature with the rounded top is Mt. Watkins. Looking up at these granite giants from Mirror Lake one can only marvel at the size and depth of the glacier that carved this valley.

To continue your walk beyond the lake, look for the horse trail on the north side of the lake at the base of the canyon wall. The trail is

marked at the parking area. The sandy, undulating trail leads you gradually away from the lake through a variety of trees including live oak, cedar, fir, maple and dogwood. At times you get glimpses of Tenaya Creek. In early spring you will cross small creeks carrying water from the cliffs above. Just less than a mile beyond Mirror Lake, a tree-crowded meadow becomes visible between the trail and the creek. Large plants, called horsetails, border the meadow and contribute to its verdant look.

Next you come to a junction where a trail leads away to the north up a steep climb to the valley rim, and Tenaya Lake and the high country beyond. Continue straight ahead, following the sign that says .5 mile to Snow Creek. Cross a small bridge that spans a tributary stream. Just .2 mile farther is the large bridge that crosses rushing Tenaya Creek. As you stand at the bridge observing the water cascading down this canyon, it is hard to imagine that this same rumbling water flows so quietly into Mirror Lake farther downstream.

After you cross the bridge, follow the horse trail shaded by a variety of trees down the south side of the creek. Try to locate the large black cottonwood tree approximately .2 mile west of the bridge on the south side of the trail (a tree identification book will come in handy). It is not a common tree along this trail, so its thickly-grooved gray bark and broad leaves are worth noting.

Along this walk there are several meadow-like areas in view. In early spring, some of these lush areas are wet enough to be called marshes or bogs.

Basket Dome, on the north canyon wall, becomes visible through the trees. Streams of water run down these granite cliffs in numerous small waterfalls each spring. Just east of Basket Dome, a small but particularly beautiful creek cascades down the cliff, drops over the overhanging rock, is caught by the wind, and blown like a cloud in the air. As you watch, you see the water splashing against the rock, collecting in a stream again to flow farther down the cliff into Tenaya Creek.

As you return again to Mirror Lake, you can look nearly straight up at the face of Half Dome from the south shore. A footbridge crosses Tenaya Creek .2 mile beyond the lake. Take this bridge back to the paved road you followed before on the approach to the lake. Stay on the road back to the bus stop or stables. In the alternative, pass the footbridge and continue on the trail as it borders the creek on the south side. The trail is similar to the one you have been traveling on and rejoins the paved road at the stone bridge just .2 mile above the shuttle bus stop.

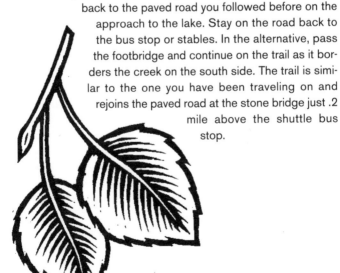

VERNAL FALL
4.6 miles | Difficult | 4 hours

The walk to Vernal Fall is the most popular hike in Yosemite Valley. It is no wonder, since the trailhead is so accessible and the view of the fall so rewarding. Each year thousands make the climb to the top of the fall to watch the water as it drops over a 317-foot cliff, polishing the rocks below and spraying the plants nearby with a fine mist.

To get to the trail, take the shuttlebus to Happy Isles Nature Center. Walk east over a stone bridge, then turn right (south) and follow along the far side of the Merced River to the large trail sign. Several hikes begin here, all of them covering the same route for one mile.

The path has been paved, although it is worn in places. Don't make the mistake of assuming that the trail will be smooth with a moderate slope the whole way. Those wearing thongs or high-heeled sandals will not be prepared for the steeper trail ahead.

The route traverses the wall of the Merced River canyon, with the cascading river often visible though the trees below. Near the beginning of the hike, a spring flows out of the rocks on the left side of the trail. This is not a reliable source of drinking water, no matter how refreshing it might look. After about .3 mile of walking, there is a bend in the trail from which you can look west to view Yosemite Falls and Glacier Point. The trail becomes steeper, although there are a few places where the trail descends briefly and you can catch your breath.

At several places along the trail you should be able to see Illilouette Fall tumbling from the top of the gorge opposite you-especially early in the season when it is full from the spring snow melt. This relatively unknown waterfall carries more water than Yosemite Falls. It makes a 370-foot drop from an elevation of 5,816 feet and then plunges down the steep gorge to meet the Merced River.

At the .8 mile mark you cross a sturdy bridge over the Merced River and are rewarded with your first view of majestic Vernal Fall. This bridge is a popular place from which to photograph the water-fall. Even if you go no further, this scenic spot makes the hike worthwhile. As you observe the spectacular view, try to absorb the power and sound of the river as it pours down the steep boulder-studded grade. Restrooms and a drinking fountain are just beyond the bridge. Because this area has been popular with bears, you should pack out any trash you may have to help protect these animals and their habitat. If you do see a bear, don't try to feed it!

The footpath continues toward the waterfall along the south side of the river. Two tenths of a mile beyond the bridge you come to the junction where the Mist Trail to Vernal Fall leaves the John Muir Trail. Either route will lead you to the top of the fall. The Mist Trail continues along the canyon wall for less than a half mile. It is quite steep—like a granite stairway—and requires a fairly strenuous climb. It is much easier for children to come back down this way. The more gradual John Muir Trail follows a roundabout route to Vernal Fall. This trail uses broad switchbacks to take you up above the waterfall on the south side; a spur trail leads back to the river and waterfall.

The John Muir Trail takes you over a sandy trail through a patchy forest. As you climb higher you are rewarded with impressive views of Glacier Point, part of the north wall of Yosemite Valley, Grizzly Peak, and occasional glimpses of the back side of Half Dome.

This trail is used by pack string and horseback parties. If a group of horses or mules needs to pass you, stand quietly to the inside of the trail where you won't frighten the animals.

One and a half miles beyond the Vernal Fall bridge you arrive at Clark Point, a crest where there is another trail junction. Thundering Nevada Fall is displayed before you. Above it stand Liberty Cap, Mt. Broderick, and Half Dome. The John Muir Trail continues 1.2 miles to the top of Nevada Fall. The other

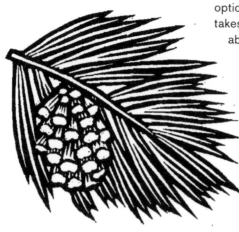

option is a spur trail that takes you down the hill just above Vernal Fall. Follow this trail down a series of rocky switch-backs. About halfway down you will get an incomparable view of Vernal Fall. You are both above the fall and in front of it giving you an unmatched perspective. Soon you reach another trail junction where your trail intersects the Mist Trail as it continues up to Nevada Fall.

If you have interest in a side trip at this point, consider walking just one-tenth mile up the trail towards Nevada Fall to the bridge over a powerful cascade. From this vantage point you can watch as the water surges through a narrow opening in the rocks, spreads out across the Silver Apron, then quietly runs into the Emerald Pool above Vernal Fall. Walking less than a half-mile far-ther up the trail you will be rewarded with some of the best views available of Nevada Fall.

From the spur junction the trail descends gradually to the Emerald Pool before it leads to the top of the fall. At the railing at the top of the fall you can watch the water drop over the cliff, crashing onto the rocks below and churning up clouds of billowing mist, while the river cascades down the canyon to Yosemite Valley.

By following the railing to the south of the fall, you can find the spot at which the Mist Trail heads down. The railing continues part-way down the side of the cliff to assist you with the narrow steps and protect you from the drop-off. The rocks can be slippery from the mist, so take time to be careful.

Heavy mist soaks hikers on the next section, and even in late summer you can expect to get wet on this walk. Children may not be as thrilled with the prospect of a drenching as adults. To ensure greater enjoyment, bring ponchos or other protective clothing for their (and your) comfort. The misty part of the trail is less than a quarter-mile but long enough to wet you to the skin if you're unprotected. Stop every so often along the walk to view the thundering waterfall from new perspectives and to note the effect of the mist on the plants around you. On a sunny day look for a rainbow at the base of the fall!

Out of the mist, you will return to the junction with the John Muir Trail. Head back down the hill one mile to the shuttlebus stop at Happy Isles.

Hikes from the Big Oak Flat and Tioga Roads

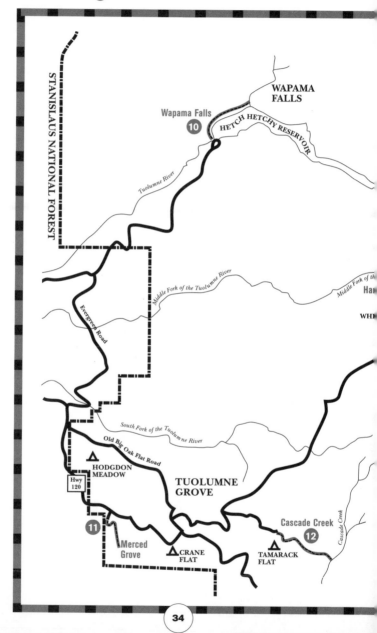

STANISLAUS NATIONAL FOREST

WAPAMA FALLS

Wapama Falls 10

HETCH HETCHY RESERVOIR

Tuolumne River

Middle Fork of the Tuolumne River

Middle Fork of the

Ha

WHI

Evergreen Road

South Fork of the Tuolumne River

Old Big Oak Flat Road

HODGDON MEADOW

Hwy 120

TUOLUMNE GROVE

11

Merced Grove

CRANE FLAT

Cascade Creek 12

TAMARACK FLAT

Cascade Creek

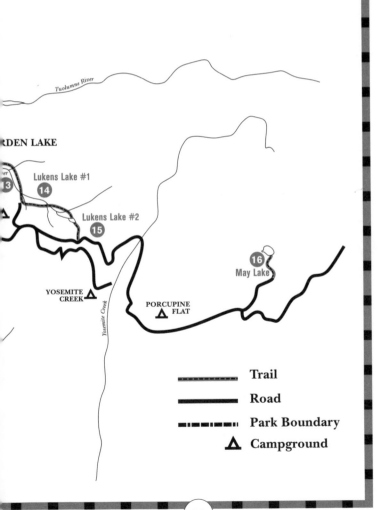

RDEN LAKE

Lukens Lake #1
13
14

Lukens Lake #2
15

16
May Lake

YOSEMITE ▲
CREEK

PORCUPINE
▲ FLAT

Tuolumne River

Yosemite Creek

------------- Trail

————— Road

■—■—■ Park Boundary

▲ Campground

WAPAMA FALLS
4 miles | **Moderate** | **3½ hours**

10

Far removed from the hustle and bustle of Yosemite Valley is another valley that is nearly as beautiful and grand—the Hetch Hetchy. A drive to this serene area is definitely worthwhile, particularly if you take the scenic hike around the north side of the reservoir to the base of Wapama Falls.

To get to the Hetch Hetchy Reservoir, leave the park through the Big Oak Flat Entrance Station and drive west on Highway 120. About a mile past the entrance station, look for a turnoff marked "Evergreen Road" to Mather and Hetch Hetchy Reservoir on the north (right) side of the road. Make the turn and follow the road sixteen miles to its end-the parking lot overlooking O'Shaughnessy Dam at the Hetch Hetchy Reservoir. This is a drive of approximately an hour and a half from Yosemite Valley. You can see Wapama Falls across the reservoir. If you travel in the early spring, you will also see Tueeulala Falls (it dries up by mid-summer) further to the west. Hetch Hetchy Dome rises out of the wooded hills beyond Wapama Falls.

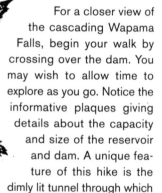

For a closer view of the cascading Wapama Falls, begin your walk by crossing over the dam. You may wish to allow time to explore as you go. Notice the informative plaques giving details about the capacity and size of the reservoir and dam. A unique feature of this hike is the dimly lit tunnel through which you pass at the end of the dam. The trail beyond is an old dirt road lined with gray (or bull) pines, which, though common in the Sierra, occur in few areas of Yosemite National Park. You can identify these trees by their long, sparse needles, which grow in uneven, spreading clumps, and by their large barbed cones.

The road you travel is flat for a short while, then crosses a stream flanked with giant California ferns. As the road begins to climb you'll encounter an incline of about a half-mile that is fairly steep for little legs. The trail is easier and more interesting beyond this section. One six-year-old described the hike as: "Extremely beautiful and a little bit hard." Notice the changing view of the reservoir as you get higher. The large dome protruding from

the forested hill across the water is Kolana Rock. To the southeast of it, Smith Peak is visible in the distance.

Before the road turns more steeply up the hill, you will see a sign for a trail branching off the road to your right. It is marked, "Rancheria Creek 6 miles." Follow this trail just over a mile as it takes you down and back up, among flowers and under trees, over rock and through grasses (and perhaps across some wet rock if you travel when Tueeulala Falls is still running) to Wapama Falls.

Here the water comes down the side of the valley wall as one fall, then divides into a series of cascades as it enters the reservoir. You can view this refreshing display from any of the four bridges that span the cascades. If you travel in the early season you are likely to enjoy, too, a shower of mist from the tumultuous fall.

There are numerous open areas on this trail where there is no protection from the sun and heat—so be prepared with adequate drinking water, sun block, and covering clothing. These open areas afford memorable views of the Hetch Hetchy Reservoir, the valley walls surrounding it, and some glimpses of the river canyon leading into the reservoir.

Be on the lookout for the poison oak that lines the trail in many places. In order to protect your skin from rash, learn to identify this plant and avoid it.

Return to the O'Shaughnessy Dam trailhead by retracing your steps.

MERCED GROVE
4 miles | **Moderate** | **3 hours**

A walk to this secluded grove gives an impression of what it might have been like for early travelers to have encountered unexpectedly the breathtaking and majestic giant sequoias.

Drive about 3.5 miles west of the Crane Flat Campground on the Big Oak Flat Road. The trailhead for the Merced Grove is on the south side of the road and is marked by a sign visible from your car.

The trail is a smooth dirt road winding through a thick forest. Park visitors could drive down this rustic road to visit the big trees until the early 1980s. Now the road is closed to the public, but on occasion you may share the route with park service vehicles.

The trail starts by cutting across the side of a forested hill. It is an easy, flat walk for a mile, then the road branches. Take the road on the left, past a gate. It immediately descends down a steep hill. Trees crowd out the sun as the road switches back and forth, taking you deeper into a canyon.

At the base of the hill, you suddenly come upon six of the giant sequoias. A small creek runs quietly between two of the trees, making a picturesque scene. Standing this close to the trees, take the opportunity to feel the spongy texture of the red bark. Perhaps you can spot some of their cones on the ground. About the size of chicken egg, the cones are smaller than you would expect for such an enormous tree.

As you continue your walk you will notice over a dozen more giant sequoias among the more common trees along both sides of the road. An old log cabin on the right side of the road once served as a ranger station, but now is closed to visitors. Beyond the cabin even more of the giant trees can be viewed from the road. Keep walking until you come to a burned area of the forest where the trail is not well-maintained. Reverse your steps to return to the Big Oak Flat Road.

CASCADE CREEK
5 miles | Moderate | 3½ hours

The historic Old Big Oak Flat Road was once a stagecoach and auto route into Yosemite Valley. Now it is a convenient trail to beautiful Cascade Creek.

This old road originally brought park visitors east from the community of Big Oak Flat, about thirty miles outside of the park. The road climbed through the Tuolumne Grove of Big Trees, past Crane Flat to Tamarack Flat, and down the rocky slope west of El Capitan to the floor of Yosemite Valley. The road beyond Tamarack Flat is closed to vehicles now, but it is still used as a broad path for hikers.

From Crane Flat, drive east on the Tioga Road. In about 3.5 miles you will come to the turnoff to Tamarack Flat campground (just before you reach the Gin Flat turnout and exhibit). Drive down this road three miles to the campground. Park at the far end of the campground where a chain separates motor traffic from foot traffic; a trail sign marks the way to Yosemite Valley.

The trail is flat or gently undulating for the first half of the walk. The trail then descends the rest of the way to Cascade Creek.

A variety of trees, including some tall Jeffery pines, shades the road. Bracken ferns line the pathway, and in several places they carpet large areas. There are also wildflowers along the way, growing profusely near creeks and in a meadow area. Boulders and expanses of exposed granite are visible on both sides of the road. Watch for a unique formation on the way—a huge, mossy, mushroom-shaped boulder on the north side of the trail.

The trail crosses two creeks. The first is Tamarack Creek, less than a half-mile along the way. One and one-half miles farther along, an unnamed creek runs across the road and flows down a ravine paralleling the road, eventually merging with Cascade Creek.

When you have walked 2.4 miles, the trail from the new Big Oak Flat Road meets the old road you've been walking on. A side trip along this trail less than fifty yards brings you back to the creek you've been following, now cascading over rocks and collecting in pools.

Return to the road and walk just one-tenth of a mile down the hill to the bridge that spans Cascade Creek.

From this bridge, watch the water as it flows down the hill, over rocks, under the bridge, and over a ledge before it disappears behind a large rock outcropping. Cross the bridge, find your way below the rock outcropping to the right, and enjoy the view of the water as it tumbles into deep pools and finally merges with Cascade Creek.

Return to Tamarack Flat by retracing your steps up the hill.

HARDEN LAKE

5.8 miles | Moderate | 4 hours

Though Harden Lake is fairly close to a major campground, it retains a secluded atmosphere and makes a pleasant hiking destination. Try it for a picnic lunch, for a refreshing romp in the water at the lake's edge, or for a little trout fishing (or all three!).

White Wolf Campground, off the Tioga Road, is the starting point for the hike to Harden Lake. Beyond the service area past the campground entrance, the dirt road is closed to public vehicles. Use this road as your trail to the lake. The route has historical significance as it was part of the original Tioga Road built in 1883 to the Tioga Mine near near Tioga Pass. Motorists used it until 1961 when the new Tioga Road was completed.

The cascading creek that parallels the trail for most of the walk is the Middle Fork of the Tuolumne River. You should see a variety of wildflowers along the trail; there are several that are found few other places in the park. In the small meadows you pass through try looking up wildflowers in your identification book.

As you near Harden Lake, a trail marked "Harden Lake .9 mi." leaves the road. Both the trail and the road lead to the lake. The trail takes you up over a small hill before approaching the lake. If you choose to continue on the road, watch for the point where it branches farther along. Keep to the right branch.

Trees surround Harden Lake, some even growing in the shallow water at its edge. Notice the graceful aspen trees across the water from the spot where you first view the lake.

If you still have energy and an adventurous spirit, walk around the lake and make your way up the slight rise on the other side. Then look for an opening in the trees and you will be rewarded with a view of the beautiful Grand Canyon of the Tuolumne River and the vast park area beyond.

Return to White Wolf Campground by retracing your steps along the route you came.

LUKENS LAKE #1

4.6 miles | Moderate | 3 hours

This is a popular hike because it is not too demanding, while giving a good sense of what backcountry walking is like. You will travel through forested areas interspersed with meadows, follow a river, and end at a placid lake.

Two trails lead to Lukens Lake from different points on the Tioga Road. This hike, the longer of the two, begins at White Wolf Campground. A sign at the parking area marks the start of the trail. Skirting the campground on the south side, the easy trail leads you east through a forest of lodgepole pines. The Middle Fork of the Tuolumne River comes into view in a few places before the trail crosses it on logs.

Less than a quarter-mile beyond the river crossing, the Lukens Lake trail joins a wider trail heading north-south; the trail north meets a path running along the rim of the Grand Canyon of the Tuolumne River (about three miles past this point). Follow the trail to the south (to the right) and continue on it as it winds east again. In the early summer, the meadows in this area are carpeted with purple shooting stars. You may want to use your camera or drawing supplies to capture their beauty. Watch for deer in the flower-filled meadows on this hike.

In the early part of the season, the trail can be muddy in places where small creeks run toward the river or where snow is melting. The forest cover becomes less dense and the ground sandier as you approach a junction with the Ten Lakes trail. Again, take the route to the right that crosses back over the Tuolumne River. If you are tired or in need of refreshment, take a break here. Lukens Lake is only about .3 miles ahead, but the trail is steeper and to the weary and hungry, the moderate incline at the end can seem difficult. Continue up the hill to the lake, passing a lush, sloping meadow visible through the trees to the right.

The shore of Lukens Lake is lined with trees on the south and west sides and edged by an open meadow on the east. The logs that jut into the water around the lake serve nicely as piers for fishermen and swimmers.

Return to White Wolf by retracing your steps.

15

LUKENS LAKE #2
1.6 miles | Moderate | 1 hour

This trail to Lukens Lake has become quite popular because it is a short route to a good fishing spot.

The trail begins on the north side of the Tioga Road, 1.8 miles east of White Wolf (or 3 miles west of the point where the road crosses Yosemite Creek). There is a parking area at this point on the south side of the road.

Just a few steps away from the road, the trail crosses a small stream, then re-crosses it in another fifty yards before it begins to head up a hill. The route parallels this little stream which is fed by snow melting in the area. By late summer, the stream will dry up. The trail follows a moderate incline up this ridge and then down its north side to Lukens Lake.

The forest you walk through is almost exclusively red fir. Notice that the small trees are covered by a thin, silvery-white bark and that the mature firs are protected by a thick, red-brown bark. Lodgepole pines grow down the back side of the hill and close to the lake. Melting snow forms a small creek in this area that runs towards Lukens Lake. The creek separates the trail from a wide meadow, and in the early summer this is a grassy bog. But as it dries it fills with wildflowers such as shooting stars, buttercups, and corn lillies.

At the west end of this pretty meadow is Lukens Lake. The trail takes you to the lake, and you can continue all the way around it (depending upon how wet the meadow is).

At the lake you can enjoy fishing, swimming, and picnicking before you return via the same trail to the Tioga Road.

MAY LAKE
2.4 miles | Moderate | 2 hours

This short hike is especially nice for the views it affords of several well-known peaks. Half Dome, Clouds Rest, Cathedral Peak, and Mt. Hoffmann all can be glimpsed from new perspectives along this sunny walk.

Look for the turnoff to May Lake on the north side of the Tioga Road, between Porcupine Flat and Tenaya Lake. Drive up this narrow road 1.8 miles to its end where there is a parking area at Snow Pond. The trail to May Lake begins across the bridge from the parking area. Youngsters will find the pond a delight with its abundance of aquatic life. From the water's edge, you should be able to watch tadpoles, garter snakes, and small fish.

The hike to May Lake is fairly popular because it is the location of a High Sierra Camp, a commercial operation of Yosemite Concession Services Corp. The trail leads you up a moderate incline, through forest, and across open granite. As you get higher you are rewarded with progressively better views of Cathedral Peak to the east and Half Dome and Clouds Rest to the south. There are a few switchbacks where the hill is steep near the end of the hike. The trail then resumes its more moderate incline for the last .2 mile approach to May Lake.

May Lake is picturesque, with bushes and flowers growing right to the clear water's edge on one side and with rugged Mt. Hoffmann rising like a tower out of it on the other. The lake is a drinking water supply so swimming is not allowed, but it is a popular spot for fishing. You might also enjoy it as a quiet setting to photograph or identify flowers and other plants. There are pit toilets and running tap water at the south end of the lake.

Return to Snow Pond by retracing your steps.

Hikes in Tuolumne Meadows

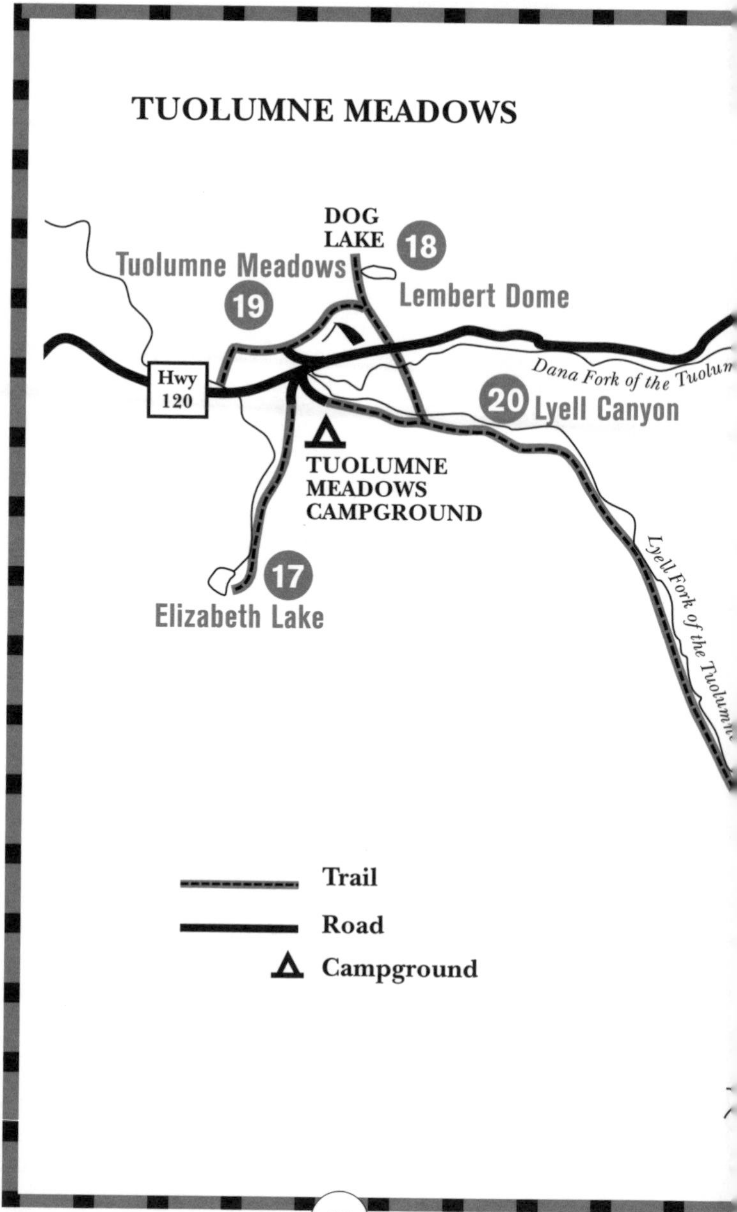

TUOLUMNE MEADOWS

DOG LAKE **18**

Tuolumne Meadows **19**

Lembert Dome

Hwy 120

Dana Fork of the Tuolum

20 Lyell Canyon

TUOLUMNE MEADOWS CAMPGROUND

17

Elizabeth Lake

Lyell Fork of the Tuolumne

—— Trail
—— Road
△ Campground

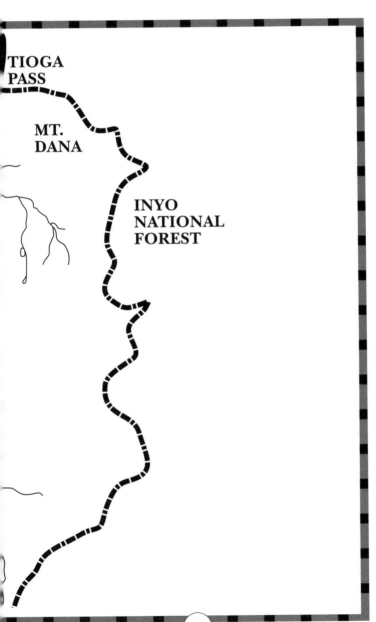

TIOGA
PASS

MT.
DANA

INYO
NATIONAL
FOREST

47

ELIZABETH LAKE
4.6 miles | Difficult | 3½ hours

The beauty of this high mountain lake makes the steep climb to it worth the effort expended.

The trail to Elizabeth Lake begins in the Tuolumne Meadows Campground. Drive or walk through the campground to the parking area outside the restroom facilities for the group camping section. A sign marks the trail from this area.

Follow the path as it heads south into a shady forest of lodgepole pines. It immediately crosses an east-west trail. Continue south and begin the ascent of the steep hill to Elizabeth Lake. Gradual switchbacks in the trail that are interspersed with short sections of level ground make the climb easier.

Mountain heather can be seen carpeting a few areas along the way each spring. By midsummer, numerous other wildflowers decorate the route. Lodgepole pine remains the dominant tree in the forest, with some mountain hemlock mixed in as you climb higher. Some large trees have fallen across the trail in places, requiring you to walk around, climb over, or even stoop under them. Several creeks cross the trail, and though they are full in the spring, they dry up as the summer progresses. You can hear Unicorn Creek off to the right, but don't see it until you are closer to the lake.

After you hike nearly two miles, the ground becomes level and the walking is easy through lush meadows lined with stunted lodgepole pines. Unicorn Creek, now in view to the right, flows away from Elizabeth Lake; a walk along its bank has become an alternate route to the lake. As you approach Elizabeth Lake you must jump across streams which are cutting deep channels through the meadow.

Looking north from this meadow area, the mountains beyond Tuolumne Meadows are in view. They make a particularly scenic backdrop for Unicorn Creek as it spills away from the lake and down the hill. To the south, jagged Unicorn Peak towers above crystal clear Elizabeth Lake, set at the base of a glacially-carved cirque.

A walk along the lake's tree-dotted shoreline rewards you with a variety of scenic displays, particularly enjoyable when they are mirrored in the water. The snow blanketing the north slope of Unicorn Peak melts slowly into the lake until fall, keeping the water cool. Breezes sometimes sweep across the lake, offering relief after a warm climb from Tuolumne Meadows.

Return to Tuolumne Meadows Campground by retracing your steps down the hill.

LEMBERT DOME
2.8 miles | Difficult | 3 hours

This hike gives you some of the benefits of scaling a peak without the strain of an all-day climb. The view from 9,450-foot Lembert Dome is well worth the effort of the hike up. Bring a map with you to identify some of the peaks you see.

Lembert Dome sits at the east end of Tuolumne Meadows. There is a parking area at its base on your left as you drive east, just beyond the bridge over the Tuolumne River. Many people mistakenly attempt to ascend the dome by going up the sloping granite that meets them at the parking area. This, however, requires the aid of ropes for safety, as the incline becomes much steeper as you climb higher.

There is an easier route up the back of the dome. You begin the walk using the "Young People's Nature Trail" that starts from the parking lot. An unmarked trail also originates here, just east of the nature trail. Both trails join about 100 yards along as they cross the granite slabs at the base of the dome.

Turn right and leave the nature trail at marker #2. The junction is marked for hikes west to Dog Lake and east to Lembert Dome. The well-worn path climbs steeply up the back of the dome through a forested area of lodgepole pine. You may cross patches of snow early in the season.

Just before you come out of the forest cover you can take a side trip to Dog Dome (located just to the north) before you head for the top of Lembert Dome. Find a spot to make an easy scramble up this sloping rock. From the top you can look down at Dog Lake and the forested hills surrounding it. Notice, too, the weather pits in the rock beneath you on the dome and the glacial erratics (random

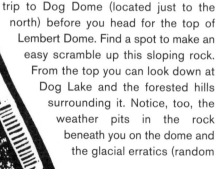

boulders) scattered about.

Return to the trail to continue the ascent of Lembert Dome. There is no prescribed path to the top once you leave the dirt and start on solid rock. Just look for the easiest route to make your way up. This requires some use of your hands as you scramble over rock in a few places. Children interested in rock climbing will especially enjoy this challenge. Once you reach the west end of the dome, gaze out at sprawling Tuolumne Meadows below you. All the major peaks in the Tuolumne Meadows area are in view, from the spikes of Cathedral and Unicorn Peaks all the way around to the red rocks of Mt. Dana at the park's entrance at Tioga Pass. A map can help you identify these peaks.

Return to the parking area by retracing your steps.

EXPLORING TUOLUMNE MEADOWS

1.5 miles | Easy | 1 hour

A walk through Tuolumne Meadows to some interesting sites will enhance your appreciation of this beautiful area. The easy 1.5 mile walk includes stops at Soda Springs, Parsons Memorial Lodge, and a bridge over the Tuolumne River.

At the east end of Tuolumne Meadows is a parking area at the base of Lembert Dome. Several hikes start here. The walk to Soda Springs begins on the same trail that leads to Glen Aulin. Walk west from the parking area on the gravel road. The road turns up the hill towards the stables; proceed straight ahead, past the gate, on the flat dirt road through the meadow. In the late spring and early summer, parts of the road may be muddy or have puddles. In midsummer the wildflowers are abundant across Tuolumne Meadows, and you will find yourself in the midst of them on this hike. The Tuolumne River meanders through the meadow, and snow-topped peaks tower above, combining to create a magnificent view. At one point you will have a choice of walking to Parsons Lodge or Glen Aulin. Opt for the route to Parsons Lodge.

Along the way, pools of bubbly mineral water spring up from under the ground. The display, known as Soda Springs, is fascinating to watch. Underground, water containing carbonic acid holds lime carbonates and metallic carbonates in solution under pressure. As the water reaches the surface, these carbonates escape in gas bubbles. Some lime is deposited around the springs, along with iron from this mineral-rich water.

Parsons Memorial Lodge is a few steps beyond the springs. The Sierra Club erected this stone building in 1915 as a memorial to Edward Parsons. Parsons was one of the most active early Sierra Club leaders and was a guide on the group's first High

Sierra trip to Tuolumne Meadows in 1901. Since its beginning, the memorial has been a reading room and library. On a sunny day it offers a cool place to sit and read or rest.

Just down the hill from the lodge is a large bridge over the Tuolumne River. This is a good spot to stop for lunch and enjoy a look at the scenery around you. Looking east, red-rocked Mt. Dana and smooth-gray Lembert Dome make a picturesque backdrop for the Tuolumne River as it flows through the meadow.

Return to the parking area by retracing your steps. (Or, if you are interested in a longer walk, follow the trail beyond the bridge one-half mile further as it leads across the meadow to the Visitor Center.)

LYELL CANYON

6-14 miles | Moderate | 4 hours minimum

As there is no predetermined destination for this hike, the most difficult thing about it is deciding when to turn around and head back. This walk takes you to some picturesque river crossings and through a quiet meadow on the floor of a wide canyon.

The trail starts at the west end of the parking lot for the Tuolumne Meadows Lodge. It leads you into a small forest and over the bridge that spans the Dana Fork of the Tuolumne River. In about .3 mile, you will reach and cross over the Lyell Fork. Take a few minutes here to enjoy this beautiful spot where the water pools and cascades under the bridge. Just beyond this bridge you come to a trail junction. Head east on the trail through the forest along the edge of some pleasant meadows. The trail undulates some, but remains fairly easy. Just .8 mile past the Lyell Fork, you come to Rafferty Creek, crossing it on a large bridge. Within a mile the trail bends to the south again. Emerging from the forest cover, you will walk through scattered areas of stunted lodgepole pines. There is a wide, grassy meadow between you and the river, which meanders through the flat canyon.

Mountain ridges rise above you on both sides—the Kuna Crest on the east, the ridge to the west, unnamed. The canyon extends for about five miles, providing you with hours of nearly effortless walking before the trail climbs out of the canyon. Walk as far as you care to, perhaps taking a detour to the river to fish, swim, wade, or relax. Return to Tuolumne Meadows by retracing your steps.

NOTES ON MY HIKES